Insects on the Move

Written by Keith Pigdon

Series Consultant: Linda Hoy

T0359536

WorldWise™
Content-based Learning

Contents

Introduction		4
Chapter 1	**Monarch butterflies: The long migration**	6
	Why do they make this journey?	6
	The monarch butterfly life cycle	8
	The autumn migration south	10
	Winter hibernation	11
	The spring migration north	12
	How do they find their way?	14
	Tracking the journey	15
Chapter 2	**The globe skimmer**	16
	What have scientists discovered?	17
	How do they do it?	18
	Why do they do it?	19
	How far do they fly?	20
Chapter 3	**Bogong moths: Looking for cooler climates**	22
	The migration	24
	Hibernation in the Alps	26
	Breeding grounds	28
Conclusion		30
Glossary		31
Index		32

Introduction

Many large animals around the world are famous for their annual **migrations**. With great anticipation, we watch for migrating whales as they swim to their feeding grounds. Flocks of birds amaze us as the fill the sky above us.

But what do we know of insects?

In North America, the monarch butterfly is well known for its long migration. Each autumn, millions of butterflies escape the cold weather in North America by flying south. In spring, they return to breed. Their migration has been regarded as the longest insect migration in the world.

Monarch butterflies in the forests in Mexico. These butterflies travel over 4,000 kilometres from North America to Mexico each year.

Small insects, long journeys

Monarch butterfly

Wing span: 8–10 centimetres
Journey: 4,800 kilometres one way

Globe skimmer

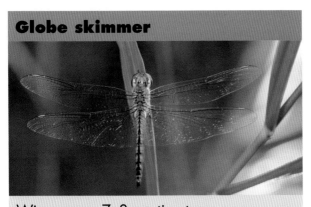

Wing span: 7–8 centimetres
Journey: 14,000–18,000 kilometres
round trip

Bogong moth

Wing span: 4–5 centimetres
Journey: 1,000 kilometres one way

Globe skimmer

But the monarch butterfly's journey is now challenged by a small dragonfly called the globe skimmer, which some scientists believe has a much longer migration than the monarch butterfly. This dragonfly needs water to breed, and scientists believe that it follows the wet weather.

The most famous insect migration in Australia is that of the bogong moth. In late spring, tens of thousands of these moths can travel up to 1,000 kilometres to the Australian Alps to shelter from the hot summer temperatures.

These small insects make very long journeys to ensure the survival of their species.

Chapter 1

Monarch butterflies: The long migration

In autumn, when the weather cools in North America, the monarch butterflies migrate south for the winter. They cannot survive in cold weather. And, their caterpillars can eat the leaves of only one type of plant – milkweeds. This plant does not grow in cold weather.

The butterflies travel a long way. They fly from the cooler parts of North America to the warmer climate of the central Mexican mountains – a journey of up to 4,800 kilometres.

The long migration of the monarch butterfly ensures the survival of the monarch species.

Many monarch butterflies travel from southern Canada and the northern states of the United States to Mexico each autumn.

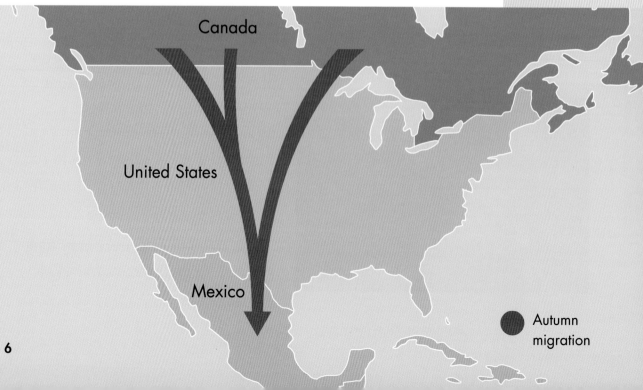

Canada

United States

Mexico

Autumn migration

Milkweeds get the "milk" part of their name because they are filled with a milky sap. Farmers treat them as weeds to be destroyed.

The monarch butterfly lays its eggs on the leaf of the milkweed plant.

A monarch caterpillar. The caterpillars are brightly coloured.

The importance of milkweeds

Monarch butterflies are totally **dependent** on a plant called milkweed. Adult monarch butterflies feed on the nectar of milkweed plants as well as other flowering plants, but their caterpillars can only eat milkweed plants.

The milkweed protects the caterpillars from predators. The sap of this plant is poisonous to many animals, but this poison does not harm the caterpillars. It protects them. It makes the caterpillars taste bitter.

The monarch butterfly life cycle

Monarch butterflies have four stages in their life cycle.

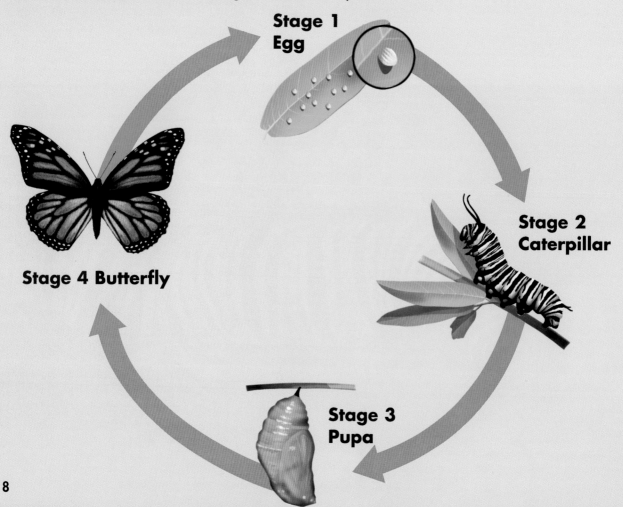

**Stage 1
Egg**

**Stage 2
Caterpillar**

**Stage 3
Pupa**

Stage 4 Butterfly

When large predators such as birds try to eat the caterpillars, they discover the terrible taste and become ill. They remember to stay away from those caterpillars in future!

This butterfly has just emerged from its pupa. Its new wings are small, so it pumps body fluid through the veins in its wings to make them bigger.

Stage 1 Egg

Monarch butterflies lay eggs on the leaves of milkweeds. A caterpillar grows inside each egg.

Stage 2 Caterpillar (Larva)

Next, the eggs hatch as caterpillars and eat the milkweed leaves. Each caterpillar eats so much that it outgrows its skin and sheds it. This is called **moulting**. As a caterpillar keeps eating and growing, it continues to shed its skin and grow new ones.

Stage 3 Pupa (Chrysalis)

At full size, the caterpillar forms itself into a pupa. From the outside of a pupa, it looks as if the caterpillar may just be resting in a special covering. But inside the pupa is where all the action is – the caterpillar is turning into a butterfly.

Stage 4 Butterfly

In the final stage, after about two weeks, the butterfly emerges from the pupa. Within about two to three hours, the butterfly will master flying and will search for food. It will also look for a mate so it can reproduce.

When its wings are dry, the butterfly flies away to find food.

9

The autumn migration south

In the autumn, the temperature in southern Canada and northern United States becomes colder, and the milkweeds that the monarch butterflies depend on begin to die. The monarchs cannot survive the cold winters of most of the United States, so they start the long journey south to Mexico, where it is warmer.

Most monarch butterflies live for two to six weeks, but the **generation** of monarchs that migrates from Canada and the northern USA to Mexico is very different. It lives for six to eight months – much longer than other monarchs.

These butterflies have fat stored in their bodies, and this gives them the energy to fly so far and to hibernate. As they fly south, they stop to eat, drink and rest. They feed on nectar from many flowers and also on water, but they do not breed.

The flying monarchs

Depending on the wind, monarchs fly at about 15 to 25 kilometres per hour for about six to eight hours a day. A monarch butterfly has been recorded flying as far as 425 kilometres in one day.

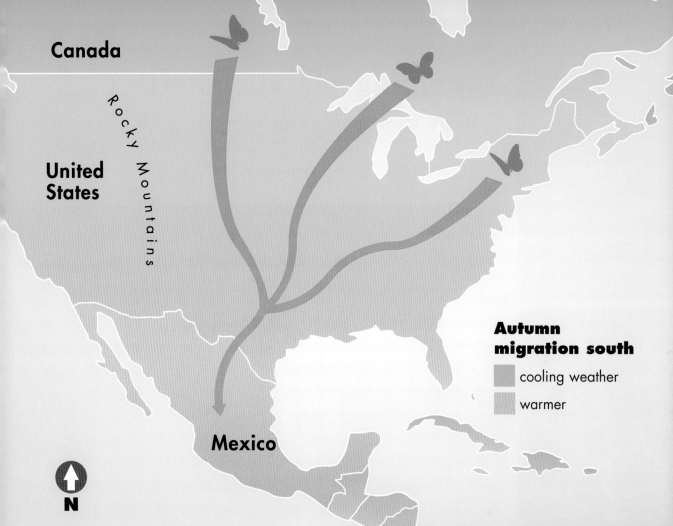

Canada

United States

Rocky Mountains

Autumn migration south

cooling weather

warmer

Mexico

N

Winter hibernation

When the monarch butterflies reach the fir forests in central Mexico, they **cluster** on the trees. They reduce their activity and they hibernate for up to six months.

They do not eat or breed. They rest in the trees and live off their body fat.

In spring, they come out of **hibernation** and the cycle starts again.

The spring migration north

In Mexico, the temperature gets warmer in March. It is spring. In the forests, monarch butterflies come out of hibernation – they need to find mates and begin laying eggs.

But milkweeds do not grow in Mexico, and so the butterflies must travel north to places such as Texas, where there are plenty of milkweeds – food for the monarch caterpillars. They mate and lay eggs. After laying eggs, these monarch butterflies from Mexico die.

After about 28 days, the new adult butterflies emerge. They are called Generation One, and they begin a new cycle of migration. They continue to fly north into warm weather where milkweeds grow. These butterflies have a short life of two to six weeks; they mate, lay their eggs and then they die.

The eggs hatch, and a new generation of monarch butterflies is born – Generation Two. They continue to fly north and repeat the cycle. They mate, lay their eggs and then they die. The eggs from Generation Two produce Generation Three, which continues to fly north towards warmer weather and milkweeds.

How far north the monarchs fly depends on how warm the summer is. If it is a long, warm summer, there will be another generation of butterflies, Generation Four and sometimes Generation Five. In autumn, this generation will make the long journey south to Mexico.

Milkweed plants

Life span of monarch butterfly generations	
Generation ① ② ③	2–6 weeks
Generation ④	6–8 months

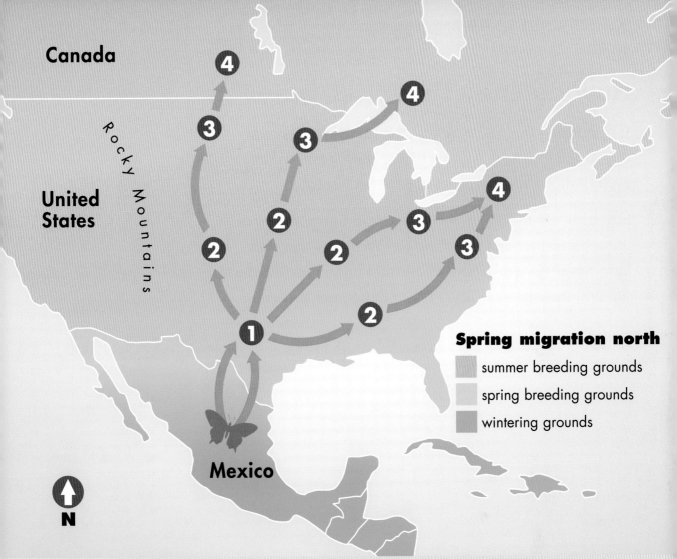

Canada

United States

Rocky Mountains

Mexico

N

Spring migration north

- summer breeding grounds
- spring breeding grounds
- wintering grounds

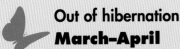 **Out of hibernation**
March–April
The butterflies in Mexico come out of hibernation and fly north. They mate, lay their eggs and die. When these eggs hatch, the butterflies are Generation 1.

 **Generations ❶ & ❷**
April–May
Generation 1 butterflies fly further north. They mate, lay eggs and die. When these eggs hatch, the butterflies are Generation 2.

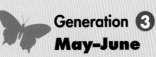 **Generation ❸**
May–June
Generation 2 butterflies fly further north. They mate, lay eggs and die. When these eggs hatch, the butterflies are Generation 3.

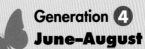 **Generation ❹**
June–August
Generation 3 butterflies continue to fly north, where they mate, lay eggs and then die. When these eggs hatch, the butterflies are Generation 4.

How do they find their way?

It is amazing that these monarch butterflies know the way to the forests in Mexico where they spend winter, even though they have never been there before.

Scientists have found it hard to explain how millions of these butterflies can find their way to places that they have never visited. They believe that monarchs use the sun and their sense of the time of day to guide them.

At the end of October each year, millions of monarch butterflies arrive in the forests in Mexico. Scientists are not sure how they know where to go.

Did you know?

Millions of monarch butterflies spend the winter in the fir forests in central Mexico each year. In 2008, UNESCO made this area a **World Heritage site** to protect the key areas for monarch butterflies.

Tracking the journey

Tracking devices like the one on this butterfly (right) help scientists learn more about the journey of the monarch butterflies.

Monarch butterflies are delicate creatures. Scientists have to be careful not to damage each butterfly as they attach a tracking device.

The oyamel fir forest in Mexico, which was made a UNESCO World Heritage site in 2008.

Chapter 2

The globe skimmer

Most dragonflies don't ever leave the pond on which they're born. But one species – the global skimmer – probably travels further than any other insect.

The globe skimmer is found throughout Asia, India, Africa, Australia and South America, and scientists now believe that this tiny insect travels long distances in search of water.

Distribution of globe skimmers

Europe

Asia

Africa

North America

South America

Australia

What have scientists discovered?

The globe skimmer is a small insect that is barely 4 centimetres long.

Most animal **migrations** can be tracked and observed by scientists. Often small radio transmitters that send regular signals to satellites are attached to animals to record their movements. But because globe skimmers are very small insects, they cannot be tagged with transmitters and many questions about their journey remain.

Nonetheless, scientists have made an interesting discovery. They have discovered that globe skimmers in different countries have similar genes, and that there is only one likely explanation. Somehow these insects are travelling distances that are extraordinarily long for their small size, breeding with each other, and creating a common worldwide gene pool that would be impossible if they did not meet.

They say that if North American globe skimmers bred with only North American globe skimmers, and Indian globe skimmers bred with only Indian globe skimmers, then the genetic profiles would be different from location to location. But this isn't the case and this suggests the mixing of genes across vast geographic expanses.

Scientists may be right about their amazing discovery, but until the globe skimmers can be identified individually, there remains some doubt. Perhaps we will know what happens sometime in the future. This is how science works.

The globe skimmer has wide, flat wings.

How do they do it?

Scientists believe that globe skimmers make the long ocean flights by gliding on the winds that blow during rainy seasons called monsoons. These dragonflies have physical adaptations that help them to make the long journey.

Their body shape and large transparent wings enable them to use the wind to carry them. They flap their wings and then glide for long periods. By gliding, they can travel incredible distances while conserving as much energy as possible.

While they are flying, they feed on **aerial plankton** and other small insects.

The globe skimmer cannot breed in dry places.

Why do they do it?

All dragonflies require fresh water to be able to breed, but many globe skimmers live in places where it does not rain all year round. Without the freshwater pools created by rain, globe skimmers cannot breed.

Scientists think that globe skimmers migrate to follow the weather. These dragonflies, in fact, have been observed crossing the Indian Ocean from Asia to Africa. It is thought that they follow the shifting rain patterns of the monsoons.

One scientist, Daniel Toaster, who worked on the globe skimmer research project, noted: "They're going from India where it's the dry season to Africa where it's the moist season, and apparently they do it once a year."

This is why these insects attempt such a perilous journey. The species depends on it. While many dragonflies will die on their journey, enough make it and the species survives.

During the monsoon season, the heavy rain creates large pools of water. Globe skimmers need pools of water in which to lay their eggs.

How far do they fly?

The round trip is 14,000 to 18,000 kilometres. Monarchs in North America travel 5,000 kilometres. If this is true, globe skimmers have the longest migration of any insect.

The dragonflies' flight patterns appear to vary. The hardiest of the dragonflies might make the trip nonstop, catching strong air currents or even cyclone winds and gliding all the way.

Others are more like puddle jumpers. If they spot a freshwater pool during their journey, they may dive earthward and use those pools to mate. After the eggs hatch and the young are mature enough to fly – which takes just a few weeks – the new dragonflies join the swarm right where their parents left off.

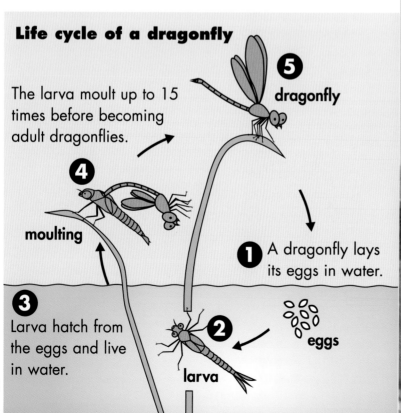

Life cycle of a dragonfly

The larva moult up to 15 times before becoming adult dragonflies.

5 dragonfly

4

moulting

1 A dragonfly lays its eggs in water.

3 Larva hatch from the eggs and live in water.

2

eggs

larva

Questions that still mystify scientists about the dragonfly migration

- Every year millions of dragonflies appear in the Maldives and the Seychelles – where have they come from?
- Are the globe skimmers seen in all these places related to each other?
- At the moment, it is impossible to attach tags to such small insects, so scientists cannot gather information.

Chapter 3

Bogong moths: Looking for cooler climates

Most bogong moths are found in eastern and south-eastern Australia, where they breed during autumn and winter.

But, adult bogong moths are unable to survive in the high temperatures of summer in this part of Australia. In late spring, the moths travel to the cool dark caves and crevices in the mountains of the Southern Alps, which provide ideal conditions to protect them from the heat.

Did you know?

The name bogong moth comes from the Bogong High Plains region in Victoria where the moths gather in large numbers over the summer.

Mount Bogong in the Australian Alps.

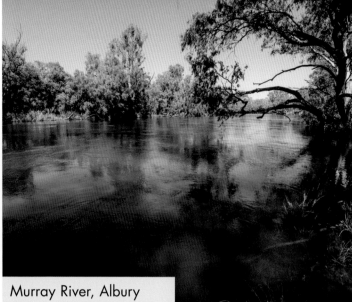

Murray River, Albury

Preserving an important cultural link

In the past, the annual **migration** of the bogong moths united families from different Aboriginal nations. There is evidence to show that bogong moths were an important food source for at least 1,000 years. The moths are up to 70 per cent fat, and a nutritious source of protein.

Up to the mid-1800s, tribes of Aborigines travelled up to the high country each summer. They roasted the moths or added them to damper. They ground the moth bodies into a paste and made it into "moth meat" cakes that would last and could be taken home.

Before they travelled to the high country, the groups would meet for a ceremony on the banks of the Murray River to celebrate the arrival of the moths. This was an opportunity to trade goods and to talk. The place where they met is called Mungabareena – the Place of Plenty Talk.

The migration

The journey from the bogong moths' breeding grounds to the mountains can be up to 1,000 kilometres long. Large swarms of moths fly during the night and rest during the day. At dusk each day, they feed on flower nectar and then continue their journey to the mountains. Scientists have found that the moths use Earth's magnetic field and important landmarks to find their way during the migration.

In spring, people in the cities and towns on Australia's south-eastern coast sometimes find bogong moths flapping around their windows, or dead on the ground or even inside buildings. The moths are attracted to the lights of cities and towns. Sometimes large numbers of bogongs are blown off course by strong winds that blow them towards the coast.

Predators

The moths are also in danger from predators during their migration. Animals such as little raven and other birds gather in large numbers to feast on bogong moths as they travel to the mountains in spring.

Did you know?

In some years, strong winds cause bogong moths to reach the large cities of Sydney and Melbourne and, more frequently, Canberra.

The currawong (left) and Richard's pipit (right) are some of the birds that prey on bogong moths.

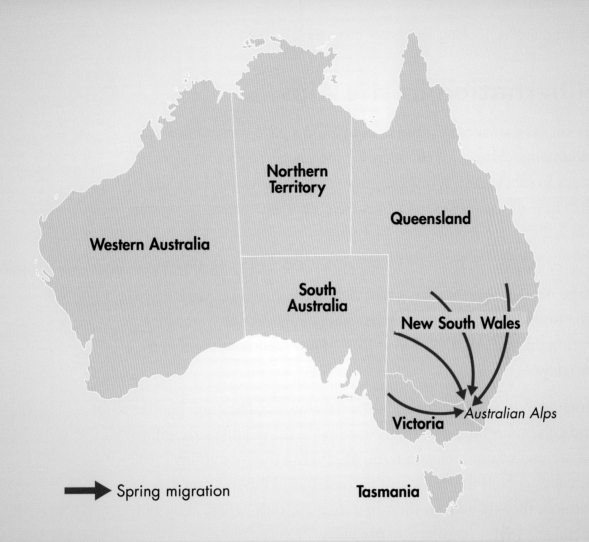

Western Australia

Northern Territory

Queensland

South Australia

New South Wales

Victoria

Australian Alps

→ Spring migration

Tasmania

Spring–Summer
November–February

The moths rest in the mountains. Here, they avoid the hot weather of the plains that would kill most of them, but many predators feed on the moths in the mountains.

Autumn
March

The moths leave the mountains, feed on nectar and migrate north or west back to the same area where they were born.

Autumn–Winter
April–August

The moths start to reach their breeding grounds, mate, lay eggs and die. The caterpillars grow, turn into pupa and then into moths. The next **generation** of moths also **reproduces** and dies.

Spring
September–October

The moths leave their breeding grounds and fly to the mountains. Flying at night, they migrate south or east towards the Alps, feeding on nectar as they travel.

Hibernation in the Alps

By the start of summer, the bogong moths have arrived in the mountains. Masses of them crowd together in rock crevices and caves to hibernate. While they rest, they do not eat. Instead, they live off the fat reserves they have built up during the winter, when they were feeding and breeding.

Each moth rests under the wings of another and so they form a large blanket against a cave wall (17,000 moths per square metre). The humidity and regular temperatures help reduce water loss during this long period of inactivity. They hibernate for about 100 days.

Bogong moths do not breed in the mountains. The food plants and conditions here are totally unsuitable for bogong caterpillars. At the end of summer, when the weather in the mountains becomes cooler, the adult moths come out of hibernation. In autumn, they fly back to their breeding grounds, where they will spend the winter feeding and breeding.

Predators

In the mountains, bogong moths are hunted by many predators. The large fat reserves that support them over the summer period makes bogong moths a key target.

Predators such as birds, lizards, spiders, pygmy possums and bats are just some of the small animals that feed on the moths while they hibernate.

A swarm of bogong moths in hibernation.

A broad-toothed rat. This animal preys on the bogong moths while they hibernate.

The powerful owl is a predator of the moths in the mountains.

27

Breeding grounds

When the bogong moths return to their breeding grounds in autumn, there are plenty of wild plants and crops for the bogong moth caterpillars to feed on.

In late spring and early summer however, the grasses and summer crops are unsuitable for the moths to eat. With the daily temperatures increasing, new generations of adult moths begin their long migration, feeding on nectar as they travel to the Southern Alps.

The bogong moth life cycle

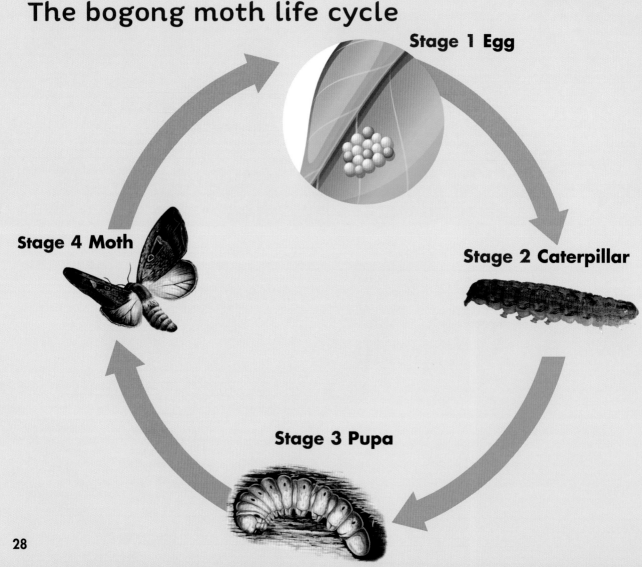

Stage 1 Egg

Stage 2 Caterpillar

Stage 3 Pupa

Stage 4 Moth

Find out more

Why are the caterpillars of Bogong moths called cutworm caterpillars?

Stage 1 Egg

The moth lays around 2,000 eggs in April and May. The eggs are laid in the soil or on plants that the caterpillars will eat.

A caterpillar grows inside each egg.

Stage 2 Caterpillar (Larva)

Caterpillars hatch from the eggs after four to seven days. They feed at night and rest during the day. Bogong moth caterpillars eat plants with broad leaves and crops such as cabbage and cauliflower.

Like all caterpillars, their main task is eating. Over a period of four months, they eat and grow. They shed their skins as their bodies grow, and grow new skins. As the caterpillars get larger, they eat the stems of low-growing plants at ground level.

Stage 3 Pupa (Chrysalis)

When they reach full size from late August, these caterpillars form themselves into a pupa or chrysalis in soil chambers under the ground. While they still look like a caterpillar, many changes are taking place inside the pupa. During the next three to four weeks, these pupas turn into adult moths and emerge from the soil chambers.

Stage 4 Moth

After the adult moths emerge, they feed on the nectar of spring flowers. Moths breed more than once if it is a good season and there is plenty of food. They do not die after laying eggs.

Conclusion

The **migration** patterns of monarch butterflies, globe skimmers and bogong moths are remarkable events. It is amazing that these insects have developed life cycles that allow them to survive the threats of seasonal changes.

It is hard to understand that insects can find their way to a place far away where they have never been. Scientists have only some explanations for how insects do this and they continue to work towards a better understanding.

Species survival

Insect species	Reason for migration
Monarch butterfly	Weather Food
Globe skimmer	Breeding
Bogong moth	Weather Food

Glossary

aerial plankton tiny plants, animals and bacteria floating in the air

cluster moving or staying close together

dependent needing and relying on something, such as a plant or animal, to survive

generation a group of animals that is born and grows up at the same time

hibernation sleeping for a long time during cold weather

migration the movement of animals from one place to another each year to find food, or hibernate, or to reproduce

moulting to shed feathers, skin or fur to make way for new growth

reproduce to produce young

World Heritage site a natural or built area or structure that is recognised as being of outstanding international importance and therefore given special protection

Index

Canada 6, 10, 16

caterpillars 6, 7, 8, 9, 12, 25, 26, 28, 29

climate 6

eggs 7, 8, 9, 12, 13, 19, 20, 25, 28, 29

forest 5, 6, 11, 12, 14

hibernate 4, 10, 11, 13, 26, 27

life cycle 8–9, 20, 28–29, 30

life span 12

Mexico 5, 6, 10, 11, 12, 13, 14

migration 4, 10–13, 15, 17,
     19, 20, 21, 23, 24–26, 28, 30, 31

milkweed 6, 7, 10, 12,

moulting 9, 20, 31

nectar 7, 10, 24, 25, 28, 29

North America 5, 6, 14, 17, 20

predators 7, 24, 25, 26, 27

pupa 8, 9, 25, 28, 29

Texas 12

threats 30

United States 6, 10, 16

wings 6, 9, 18, 26